The Four Seasons
Spring

Teachers' Resource Book

STAGE ONE

© 1997 Channel Four Learning Limited
All rights reserved

Channel Four Learning Limited
Castle House
75-76 Wells Street
London W1P 3RE

Written by Shirley West
Adapted for Channel Four Learning by Pam Land
Edited by Malcolm Ward
Designed by Mark Dempsey
Illustrated by Sarah Dempsey

ISBN 1862152403

March

'March brings breezes

sharp and chill,

Shakes the dancing daffodil.'

March is named after **Mars**, the Roman god of war. This month is known for its strong winds.

The season of spring begins on the date when the days and nights are of equal length, about 21 March. It marks the end of the sleepy winter and the beginning of new life.

The word 'spring' comes from an old Anglo-Saxon word meaning 'rising'. At this time, the sun rises higher in the sky each day, the weather grows warmer and the days lengthen.

New life beginning

Millions of birds fly northwards to feed and breed. Some fly huge distances and must fatten up before they make long, tiring journeys. Stored-up body fat gives even the smallest bird the energy to cross large tracts of sea without a meal.

After migrant birds reach breeding grounds, each species claims a special patch of land, and the male sings to scare off rival males and win a female mate. Each pair of birds then builds a nest. In this the female lays her eggs, then sits on them for weeks to keep them warm until they hatch.

After waking up from hibernation, male frogs and toads lie in the water croaking to attract a mate. When a female swims near, a male seizes her around the middle and fertilises the eggs as she releases them. Once paired, a female frog or toad lays many hundreds of tiny eggs surrounded by a clear jelly, called 'frogspawn'. After a few days, frog and toad eggs hatch into tiny legless tadpoles.

Spring flowers

As spring sunshine warms the soil, the spring rains moisten it, and plants start to grow. Some flowers grow from tiny seeds, taking food and water from the soil, and energy from the sunlight. Other flowers, such as bluebells, crocuses and daffodils, grow from bulbs, which contain food stored from the year before. Gardens that have looked quite dead and bare all winter come alive with flowers, and farmers start to sow seeds of crops, such as wheat, that ripen later in the year.

A Change in the Year

It is the first mild day of March:
Each minute sweeter than before
The redbreast sings from the tall larch
That stands beside our door.

There is a blessing in the air,
Which seems a sense of joy to yield
To the bare trees, and mountain bare,
And grass in the green field.

By William Wordsworth

Spring throughout the world

All over the world, people celebrate spring festivals.

In **China**, the spring festival is called **Ch'ing Ming**, meaning 'Pure Brightness'. It is one of the oldest festivals. People sweep their ancestors' graves, eat special meals, and kindle hearth fires.

In **England**, morris dancing is popular in some areas in springtime. It is thought to come from the sacrificial spring dances that took place all over Europe over two thousand years ago.

The Britannia Coconut Dancers of Bacup, Lancashire, England, blacken their faces, wear white barrel skirts and black breeches. They are led by the whiffler, who whips away winter and ill fortune.

Most morris dancers wear bells, but the Britannia Coconut Dancers wear little discs of wood which they attach to their hands, knees and belt and clap together.

The Brampton Morris Men perform in their town of Oxten on the spring bank holiday. They are accompanied by the traditional fiddler, the fool with the bladder on a stick, and a swordbearer. The swordbearer has a large plum cake on his sword, pieces of which he distributes for luck.

In **India**, the festival of **Holi** is held by Hindus in late March or early April at the time of the Indian spring harvest. Fire and bright colours are the distinctive features of this celebration. (See page 10.)

Sikhs celebrate **Hola-Mohalla**; this is a time for sport and physical games at a fair which lasts three days.

In **Iran**, which is a Muslim country (formerly Persia), **No-Ruz** or New Year's Day, is the first day of spring. The observance is a very old one, dating back to old Persia and pre-Islamic times. The old Persian religion was Zoroastrianism, named after its founder Zoroaster. Ahura Mazda was believed to be the supreme god.

The week before the festival begins **kahneh takani** (the house-shaking, or cleaning) takes place. A day or two before No-Ruz the whole family goes to the public bath.

When the sun crosses the equator the new year begins. Families, bare-footed and dressed in their new clothing, gather together around a table. On the table are placed the bowls of growing cereal and a tray with at least seven foods beginning with the Persian letter S **(haft sin)**, which are symbols of the goodness of Allah:

sabzeh	herbs
serkeh	vinegar
seeb	apple
sir	garlic (to chase away the evil spirits)
somaq	a crystalline lemon-tasting spice (a symbol of good life)
samanoo	a sweet pudding
sekeh	gold or silver (a symbol of wealth)

For each member of the family there is a lighted candle and, if possible, a goldfish in a glass bowl. It is believed that at the moment the new year changes, the fish turns over in the water. Then the gun or cannon goes off, and each person says, 'May your new year be blessed!'

The last Wednesday before No-Ruz is known as **Chahar Shanbeh Sori**. On this day, people light small bonfires. Everyone jumps over the fire singing, 'Take away my yellow colour, I'll take your reddish hue,' which means the end of winter drabness and the beginning of summer warmth. The children receive gifts, a toy, a coin, jewellery, a plant or a flower.

In **North India** and **Pakistan**, the spring festival is called **Baswant**, which in Sanskrit means yellow, the sacred colour of India and a symbol of spring. Couples in love make this a special day of the year, as Valentine's Day is in Britain. Everyone wears yellow in some part of their clothing. The family fasts until noon and places an offering of food and white flowers before the image of the goddess of learning, **Saraswati**. It is considered to be a holy day for young children to start school. The main meal of the day is served with yellow rice specially cooked for the occasion.

This is also the season for kite flying. Families fly kites of coloured tissue paper and bamboo. For fighting kites, the first hundred feet of the kite string is often covered with a glue, holding ground glass so that during the kite fight it can cut the string of another kite whose string it crosses. Kites that fall to the ground are captured.

The **Japanese** spring festival is called **Setsubun** or 'Change of Season' and is celebrated on 3 February. Ceremonies in homes and temples take place. Roast beans are scattered around in the belief that evil spirits will be driven away, allowing the new season to start well.

In **Russia**, the farewell festival to the winter is called **Maslenitsa**. These celebrations last for a whole week and follow a strict order:

Monday:	meeting
Tuesday:	flirting, games and playing
Wednesday:	treats and pancakes
Thursday:	onslaught, plays
Friday:	party for mothers-in-law
Saturday:	sitting and speaking
Sunday:	the farewell day

During Maslenitsa, carnivals, games, walking competitions and the burning of straw scarecrows take place.

Pancake Day

Pancakes are associated with the day before Lent: Shrove Tuesday. Traditionally, this is the day for eating pancakes. The custom dates from the days before refrigeration when foods such as eggs, butter and oils had to be used up before the Lenten fast began.

Pancakes

Mix a pancake,
Stir a pancake,
Pop it in the pan;
Fry the pancake,
Toss the pancake,
Catch it if you can.

By Christina Rossetti

Pancake Day race in Olney

This race is exclusively for women no younger than sixteen. Each competitor must wear a skirt with an apron over it and a scarf on her head. She must carry a hot frying pan in her hand, with a pancake ready for tossing.

The origin of the race is believed to come from a woman in Olney who was trying to use all her eggs before Lent began. She was interrupted by the shriving bell calling all to receive absolution, and ran to church with frying pan and batter in her hand. The bell is known locally as the **Pancake Bell**.

Then, over twenty years ago, the villagers of Olney were challenged to a race by the people of Liberal, in Kansas, USA.

The Olney women won and this led to the institution of a pancake race as an annual event on both sides of the Atlantic.

There was a time when children raced from door to door on Shrove Tuesday, cadging treats from the neighbours and chanting this rhyme:

Pancakes!
Pancakes!
Don't let the pancakes
Frizzle away.

Today the boys at Westminster School, London still scramble for the pancake on Shrove Tuesday, chanting:

Pancakes!
Pancakes!
Pancake Day!
If you don't give us any
We'll all run away.

Cooking

Making pancakes
Page 36 gives a recipe for pancakes.

Crêpes
The French call their pancakes **crêpes**. They love to eat their crêpes with jam, butter or cheese. According to an old custom, it is believed that if you flip the crêpes quickly in the skillet with one hand and you have a coin in the other hand, you will have good luck and money all year long! There is a recipe for crêpes on page 37.

Blini
In Russia during Shrovetide, which they call **Myas Ianitza** ('Butter Milk') they eat pancakes called **blini**, made with yeast. These are served with melted butter and sour cream. There is a recipe on page 36 for blini.

Bao Bing
The Chinese eat very thin pancakes called **bao bings**. They have nothing to do with any religious celebration. They are the inspiration for spring rolls sold in all Chinese restaurants and take-aways.

Phuluka
There are several types of wheaten pancake called **phulukas** made in India. The recipe on page 39 is for one of them. In India, a pan called a **tawa** is used instead of a frying pan.

Ash Wednesday
Between 4 February and 11 March

Ash Wednesday is the first day of Lent. Traditionally, it was a time for penance and fasting in memory of Christ's fast in the desert. In the Roman Catholic church, the congregation receive a cross marked on the forehead with the ashes obtained from the burning of the palms used on the previous Palm Sunday in memory of Christ. The small crosses made from strands of palm fronds are an old symbol of grief and mourning.

Things to do

French children made a little paper nun to mark off the Lenten weeks.

Paper Nuns

You will need:
card, crayons

Method
1. Draw and cut out an outline of a nun on the card. Give her seven feet, one for each week during Lent. All feet must be facing the same way. Her arms and hands are always folded in prayer.
2. Don't give her a mouth because this is a reminder that lent is a time of fasting. Turn one little foot under her gown as each week passes.

Before calendars, people invented ways to mark off the passing weeks of Lent. Greek children made a **kukaras**. This is made from a large potato tied with ribbon with seven feathers stuck in it, one for each week of Lent. They are hung in the doorway of the kitchen. For each week that goes by, one feather is pulled out.

The Four Seasons • Spring

No-Ruz

No-Ruz begins on 21 March, lasting twelve days. See page 4 for details.

Things to do

Make a Necklace from Papier Mâché

You will need:
newspaper, glue, paint, thin stick, varnish, thread

For the paste, use any of the following:
1. 3 cups of water mixed with 1 cup of flour.
2. 1 cup of wallpaper paste mixed with 3 cups of water.
3. 2 cups of white glue mixed with 1 cup of water.

Method
1. Add strips of torn newspaper to the paste until the mixture is manageable. Squeeze away any excess water.
2. Make beads of all kinds of shapes and sizes from the papier mâché pulp. Use a thin stick to poke holes through the beads while they are still wet. When the papier mâché is dry, paint the beads and varnish them. String the beads to make the necklace.

Other ways to make necklaces
You can also make necklaces by painting and then threading pasta tubes, or by drying out watermelon pips by cooking in a slow oven for an hour, then painting and threading them. The pips can also be used to make a collage.

Planting the Sabzeh

Two weeks before the No-Ruz celebration, each family plants the Sabzeh: wheat or barley seeds. If you don't have wheat or barley, try planting some lentil, watercress, sunflower or grass seeds.

You will need:
seeds, plate, sponge or cotton wool

Method
1. Place a damp sponge or cotton wool on a plate and sprinkle with seeds. Water a little each day and soon you will have sprouts.
2. On the last day of the celebrations, you must throw out the bowls of green into some running water, a sign that all illness, bad luck, ill feeling and family quarrels are cast away.

Holi

At the full moon in March or April

Holi is a famous and very popular Hindu spring festival in India. It celebrates the arrival of spring flowers, when the main crops are almost ready for the spring harvest. The festival lasts anything from three to five days and is known as the 'festival of colour'.

Holi usually begins with the lighting of bonfires which have been built by everyone. People light their household fires, and then the community fire is kindled by a Brahmin priest. The ripening of the first wheat and barley crop is celebrated by being offered to the fire, and the roasted barley is eaten. The ashes of the fires are marked on the forehead to bring good luck in the year ahead.

After the bonfires comes the throwing of colour. People throw coloured water and red powders over friends or anyone who passes by. It is a happy celebration, everybody dances and has great fun. Processions of floats carrying statues of the gods line the streets.

Holi is named after the goddess Holika. During the festival, people burn the image of Holika as a symbol that good has defeated evil. This is often followed by the burning of rubbish, to show that past wrong-doing is forgiven.

The Story of Holi

There was once a very cruel King called Hirnakashyah who had a son called Prahlad. Prahlad was very good and always prayed to the god Vishnu, which made his father very angry. The king tried very hard to make his son give up his belief in Vishnu.

So the king ordered his sister Holika to take Prahlad in her arms and for both of them to walk into the burning fire. The plan was that Prahlad would die and Holika would be saved because she was protected by the god of flames. What the king did not know was that the god's charm over Holika didn't work for one hour during the day. The hour chosen for lighting the fire just happened to be that very hour. When the flames leapt up, Holika died and Prahlad was saved by Vishnu.

Prahlad was so sorry for Holika that he promised to name a festival after her. So now we have the festival of Holi.

Things to do

Holi is a celebration of colour. In tie-dyeing the children can have fun with different colours and shapes.

Tie-Dyeing

You will need:
white fabric, a few pebbles or a stick, string, a bowl, dye, water.

Method
1. Tie various knots with string around the fabric by either tying sections around the pebbles, or twisting the cloth round a stick and tying with string.
2. Put some dye in the water. Place the fabric in the bowl for about 5 minutes. Take out, rinse and then dry.
3. In order to make another colour, tie the knots in different places and repeat steps 1 and 2. If mixing colours, begin with the lightest.

Icing Sugar Picture

For the bright fiery pictures exploding with colour, try first coating the paper with icing sugar paste to make sugar pictures. Remember this activity can get quite sticky!

You will need:
icing sugar, water, red, yellow and orange paint, paper

Method
1. Mix the icing sugar and water together to the consistency of runny paint. Paint the sugar icing quite thickly all over the paper for a good effect.
2. Dip a paint brush into the paint and allow it to drip, or lightly shake it over the paper. The paint will disperse slowly into the sugar icing creating a fire effect.

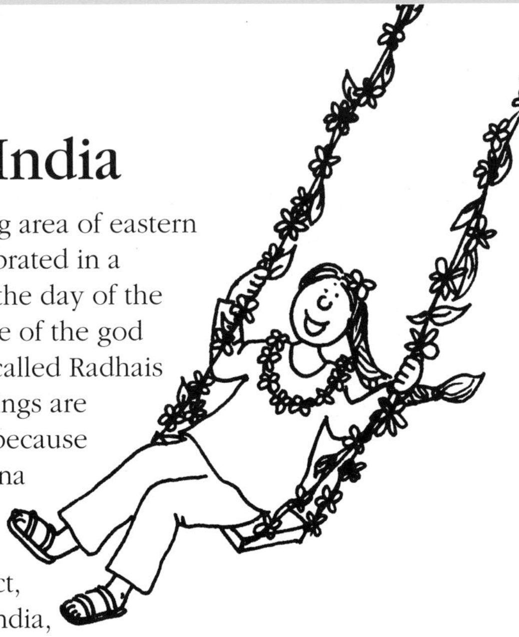

Eastern India

In the rice-growing area of eastern India, Holi is celebrated in a different way: on the day of the full moon, the love of the god Krishna for a girl called Radhais is re-enacted. Swings are made of flowers, because Radhais and Krishna were said to have played together on a swing. In fact, in some parts of India, the festival of Holi is primarily a joyful celebration of this love. The throwing of the coloured powder is seen as a remembrance of their playful frolics.

Rice

Since ancient times, rice has been the most commonly used food grain for a majority of the people of the world. Properly cultivated, rice produces higher yields than any other grain with the exception of corn; although the total area planted in rice is far smaller than that devoted to wheat – the world total is about one-third less – the rice crop feeds a far greater proportion of the world's population.

Throughout much of the world, rice is harvested by hand, using knives or sickles. The stalks are cut, tied in bundles, and left in the sun to dry.

Rice is usually eaten as milled whole grain. Cooked rice can be flaked or puffed for breakfast food and is used in prepared baby foods. Rice flour, prepared from broken grain, is used in the baking and confectionery industries.

Things to do

A Rice Picture

Making pictures with coloured rice is fun to do.

You will need:
paper, rice, red, yellow and orange food colouring, water, three small bowls.

Method
1. Mix the food colouring into separate bowls with water.
2. Divide the rice into the bowls and soak for at least an hour, then allow to dry. You can speed this process up by putting the rice in a low-heated oven.
3. Make a collage with the differently coloured rice.

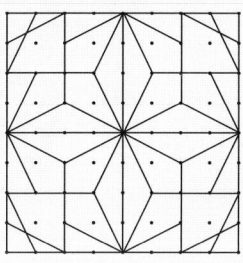

Cooking with Rice

There are several simple recipes for cooking with rice. One of the simplest with children is **rice biscuits**. **Phirni** is a traditional Indian sweet made from rice and milk, and decorated with fruit and nuts. You will find more details on page 38.

Rangoli Patterns

Rangoli patterns are used by Hindu and Sikh families to decorate their homes during festivals. Some are pictorial, while others are geometrical and abstract. Patterns are often made from food-stuffs, such as rice, lentils, split peas and seeds. These works of art are often created on the door step or in the entrance of the home so that visitors to the home have to pass over the design and therefore have good luck. Rangoli patterns are best designed on dotted paper.

Method
1. Using a square grid draw in the horizontal and vertical lines of symmetry.

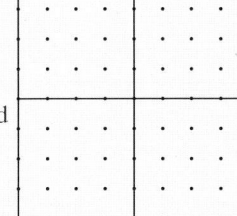

2. Join up some of the dots in one of the quaters. Not too many or it will be too complicated.

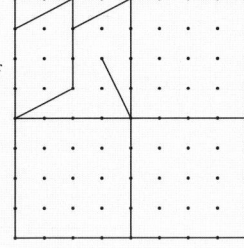

3. Reflect the lines drawn in one quater into the other three quaters, using both the vertical and horizontal axes. A small mirror may be useful.

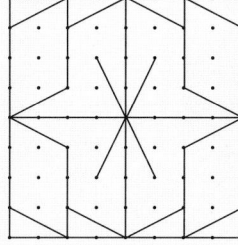

4. Draw the two diagonals in the large, original square. Reflect your lines in these diagonals. Now use colours.

Mother's Day

*'On Mothering Sunday,
above all other,
Every child should live
with its mother.'*

Fourth Sunday in Lent

Mothering Sunday used to be the one day in Lent when feasting and games were allowed. People living in villages that didn't have a church of their own would journey on that day to the nearest 'Mother' church. Later another tradition began. Servants or other young people who worked away from home were given the day off in order to visit their parents, and to take a cake or a bunch of flowers to their mother. But this custom soon died out.

In the USA, Canada and New Zealand, Mother's Day falls on the second Sunday in May.

On 9 May 1906, a Miss Anna Jarvis of Philadelphia lost her mother. On the first anniversary she invited a friend to visit her and she suggested that one day a year should be set aside for mothers. She arranged a special church service and asked everyone to wear a white or coloured carnation in honour of her mother. Coloured carnations indicate that a person's mother is living. The custom spread and in 1913 the Senate and the House of Representatives officially dedicated this day to the memory of mothers.

During the Second World War (1939–45), the American servicemen would often adopt their British hostesses as 'mothers' and on this day give presents and flowers to show their appreciation of the hospitality they enjoyed. And so the custom of Mother's Day was introduced to Britain.

Things to do

Mother's Day Picture

You will need:
thick card, a clear plastic sleeve, dried flowers

Method
1. Glue the flowers carefully to the inside of a clear plastic sleeve.
2. Cut out a border from thick card and decorate.
3. Glue the picture onto the border.

Mother's Day Card with Pressed Flowers

You will need:
flowers, white card, blotting paper, felt tips, heavy books

Method
1. Put the flowers between two sheets of blotting paper so they do not touch. Allow to dry for at least 4 weeks pressed by the heavy books placed on top.
2. Write a message in the card.
3. Glue the flowers onto the front of the card.

The word perfume comes from the Latin *per fumum* meaning 'through smoke', describing the burning of incense, which the Romans did to please the gods.

Making Perfume

You will need:
flowers, jar, orange and lemon peel, bay leaf, foil, water

Method
1. Put the flower petals in a jar with some pieces of dried orange and lemon peel, and a bay leaf. Cover with water.
2. Fix some foil over the jar with a rubber band and punch small holes in the foil.
3. Allow to stand for a few days and then drain the water.

The Four Seasons • Spring

Oranges and Lemons

Last day in March

In medieval days, barges carrying fruit from the Mediterranean landed at the wharves just below the churchyard of St Clement Dane in east London. The tenants of Clement's Inn charged porters a toll to carry oranges and lemons across their property to nearby Clare Market. Now, on the last day of March, children gather at the church to attend a service and they receive presents of fruit.

A new bell was added making twelve in all, so that the traditional Orange and Lemons tune could be played more accurately than before. The original bells were damaged by the Second World War air raids in 1940–41.

It is said that during public executions, prisoners were led along the streets to the tolling of the bells; hence: 'Here comes a chopper to chop off your head.'

Oranges and Lemons

'Orange and Lemons'
said the bells of St Clements.
'You owe me five farthings,'
said the bells of St Martin's.
'When will you pay me?'
said the bells of Old Bailey.
'When I grow rich,'
said the bells of Shoreditch.
'Pray, when will that be?'
said the bells of Stepney.
'I'm sure I don't know,'
said the great bell of Bow.
Here comes a candle to light you to bed,
Here comes a chopper to chop off your head.
Chip-Chop-Chip-Chop,
The last man is dead.

Things to do

Orange and Lemon Prints

You will need:
oranges and lemons, paper, orange and yellow paint, two flat containers for the paint

Method
Cut the fruit in half. Put some paint in each of the containers. Dip the fruit into the paint and make patterned prints on the paper.

Orange and Lemon Biscuits

Orange and Lemon biscuits are easy to make. Why not make home-made squash. Both recipes are on page 40.

Pesach
Late March or Early April

The Pesach Festival

Pesach is the Jewish festival of freedom. It is called Passover in English.

This eight-day festival is the time for spring cleaning. Once this is done the mother of the family hides pieces of bread called **hametz**, which is ordinary bread. On the evening before Passover, the children search the house for the pieces of hametz as ordinary bread is not allowed at Passover time. If any crumbs are found, the room has to be cleaned all over again.

The following morning, the whole family goes into the garden and the father places the hametz on a piece of paper and sets it alight, saying a prayer asking God to recognise that they have done their best to remove all the hametz.

A different set of kitchen utensils is used during this period, including washing-up bowls, tea towels, and anything else that comes into contact with food. The kitchen must be scrubbed clean.

The only food that is allowed to be eaten throughout Passover is called **kosher**, which means that it has been blessed by the rabbi. On the table are found foods with a special significance.

The Haggadah

A family ceremony known as the **seder** is held on the first two nights of the festival. The story of the Exodus from Egypt is retold and special foods are eaten to mark the occasion. The ceremony follows the same order in every house, and this is taken from the **Haggadah**, the Pesach order of service.

When everyone is gathered round the table, the youngest child asks some questions starting with: 'Why is this night so different from all other nights?'

The head of the house reads the answer from the Haggadah: 'Because we were the slaves in Egypt, and now we are free.'

Then the full story of the exodus continues in word and song.

The Special Night

This is a special night.
Everything must be right.

Clean the hametz from all the cupboards.
Search in every corner.
Cook special foods and then set the table.
Everything in order.

Traditional Food for the Seder Table

Bitter herbs, like watercress or horseradish, are a reminder of the harshness of slavery.

Karpas, which is a green plant like parsley, is a symbol of springtime and hope.

Charoses is chopped apple prepared to resemble the mortar and bricks used to build the ancient Egyptian cities.

A shankbone, symbolic of the sacrificial Pascal offering, is set beside an egg.

Roasted egg represents the festival sacrifice brought to the temple and is the symbol of mourning for the destroyed temple.

Salt water marks the tears shed by the slaves and the crossing of the Red Sea.

A plate of matzos recalls the hasty flight of the Israelites from Egypt.

Four cups of wine must be drunk as a reminder of the four promises made by God to redeem Israel.

A special cup of wine is poured for the Prophet Elijah, who is thought to visit each Jewish home on this night, and the door is opened for the prophet to enter. As the seder comes to an end, everybody eats a last piece of matza and thanks God for the special gift of freedom.

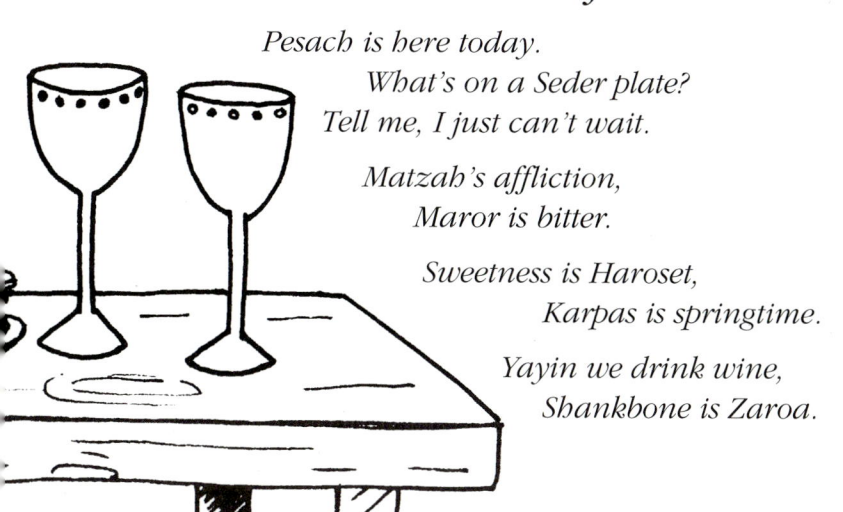

Wherefore is it Different?

Wherefore is this night different
From all other nights?
That on all other nights we eat
Either leavened or unleavened bread,
While on this night it must be unleavened bread.

Wherefore is this night different
From all other nights?
That on all other nights we eat
Any species of herbs,
While on this night we eat bitter herbs.

Wherefore is this night different
From all other nights?
That on all other nights we do not immerse
The herbs we eat
Even once,
While on this night we do it twice.

Wherefore is this night different
From all other nights?
That on all other nights we eat
Either sitting or leaning,
While on this night we all lean.

The Haggadah of Passover
Pesach is Here Today

Pesach is here today.
What's on a Seder plate?
Tell me, I just can't wait.

Matzah's affliction,
Maror is bitter.

Sweetness is Haroset,
Karpas is springtime.

Yayin we drink wine,
Shankbone is Zaroa.

Listen to King Pharaoh

Oh listen, Oh listen
Oh listen, King Pharaoh,
Oh listen, Oh listen,
Please let my people go.
They want to go away,
They work too hard all day.
King Pharaoh, King Pharaoh,
What do you say?

'No, no, no I will not let them go.
No, no, no I will not let them go.'

The story of Moses

The people of Israel came to live in Egypt, where they lived and worked as free people.

Then one day a new Pharaoh came to rule and he frightened the people of Israel by ordering all their new-born sons to be killed. A woman named Yocheved did not want her son to die so she asked her daughter Miriam to set him afloat in a basket on the River Nile. The basket was later found by the Pharaoh's daughter. She took the child home and called him Moses.

When he grew up he became a shepherd. While he was looking after the sheep, Moses came across a bush which seemed to be on fire. It was burning, but it did not turn to ash. Moses heard the voice of God telling him to go to Pharaoh and tell him to free the people from slavery.

So Moses went to Pharaoh several times to ask him to free the people of Israel. Each time Pharaoh would agree but then later he would change his mind. God in his anger cursed the Egyptians with many plagues. Finally, after nine plagues, Moses told Pharaoh that if he did not let the people of Israel go, a tenth and most terrible plague would be brought on the Egyptians. Pharaoh was frightened and told Moses to leave with his people.

The people were in such a hurry to leave, they did not have enough time to let their bread rise. They took the bread with them to bake on the way.

Moses led all the people out of Egypt to the Red Sea. There Moses touched the waters with his rod. A great miracle happened. The water spread apart so that the Israelites could pass through on dry land and walk to freedom.

Ever since then, Jewish people all over the world have celebrated at the time of Pesach.

Things to do

A Seder Plate

Painting and drawing activities at this time could focus on the story of the Exodus. Use red crêpe paper to represent the parting of the Red Sea.

You will need:
a paper plate, paper cut into five circles, egg shells, parsley, watercress, small pieces of brown paper rolled into balls (representing charoses, which is the mortar and bricks), a circle cut from silver foil to represent the salt water

Method
1. Glue some crushed egg shell, parsley, watercress and brown balls on each of the circles. Draw a bone on the last circle.
2. Glue the silver circle in the middle of the plate.
3. Glue the other symbols round the plate.

Pesach Frog Game

One of the plagues was frogs. At the Yavneh Nursery in Brighton the children play a frog game at Pesach time.

You will need:
A4 card, die, green plant

Method
1. Cut out four 30cm frog shapes and colour or paint these green.
2. Cut out 48 circles 2cm (1") in diameter. In the first circle put one dot, in the second put two dots, and so on until you reach six; then repeat.
3. Glue the six circles from one to six on the frog.
4. Divide the remaining circles amongst the four players, making sure they have one of each number.
5. Each child takes a turn at throwing the die. If they throw a number 5, for example, they have to match their circle with five dots with the circle on the frog until their frog is complete.

Cooking

During Passover, orthodox Jewish families do not eat anything that contains a raising agent. At this time recipes which use potato flour or fine matzo meal are popular.
Matzo puddings and pesach rolls are good examples of Jewish food eaten at Passover time. See page 39 for the recipes.

Hot Cross Buns

The Hare and the Tortoise

A rabbit raced a turtle,
You know the turtle won.
And Mister Bunny came in late,
A little hot cross bun!

Hot cross buns are small cakes with a cross on the top which divides the bun into four sections. The buns date back to Roman times when they were eaten as part of the spring celebrations, the four sections representing the four phases of the moon. As part of the Easter festival, the cross on the bun is now taken to symbolise the cross of Christ.

In days gone by, hot cross buns were believed to have holy powers. If you hung one from the ceiling, the house and all within would be protected. If someone was ill, you had to grate a small amount into warm milk or water. This was thought to cure most ailments. It was believed that if the bun went mouldy, then disaster would strike the house during the coming year.

Today, hot cross buns are traditionally eaten on Good Friday, the day of the Christian commemoration of the death of Jesus Christ, observed on the Friday before Easter. Originally, it was a day of fasting in preparation for the unitive celebration of the death, resurrection and exaltation of Jesus; no liturgy was held on that day. In the 4th century, at Jerusalem, a procession was staged from Gethsemane to the sanctuary of the cross, followed by readings about the passion. This was the beginning of the Good Friday observance as it is now known.

The good luck bun was supposed to hang from the ceiling from one Good Friday to the next.

A hot cross bun called the Widow's Son has been hung in a public house in the London Docklands every Good Friday since the early 19th century.

The Widow's Bun commemorates a poor widow who originally lived on the site now occupied by the pub. Every Good Friday she baked a hot cross bun for her sailor son, who, alas, never came home. Part of the agreement when the pub was built was that a sailor should hang a bun each year in memory of the widow's devotion.

Hot Cross Buns

Hot cross buns, hot cross buns!
One-a-penny, two-a-penny,
Hot cross buns!
If you have no daughters,
Give them to your sons.
One-a-penny, two-a-penny,
Hot cross buns!
But if you have none of these little elves,
Then you may eat them yourselves.

Things to do

Bun Game

Why not hang buns around the room? The children can have fun trying to eat them with their hands behind their backs.
'Hang a bun by a string
And good luck it will bring!'

Cooking Hot Cross Buns

Page 37 gives a recipe for hot cross buns. Making hot cross buns is hard for young children, so adult help is needed. Alternatively, children could compare different shop-bought ones and 'test' for the most authentic, fruitiest, spiciest, largest, heaviest, and so on, and write a 'value for money' consumer report on them.

Easter

Between 22 March and 25 April

Easter Throughout the World

Easter celebrates the resurrection of Jesus Christ after his death on the cross on Good Friday. It may fall on any of a range of days in March or April because it is kept in original relation to the Passover date, which varies with the phases of the moon. The word 'Easter' comes from **Eastre**, the goddess of light and spring.

In **Australia**, Easter falls at the end of summer, but they still hide Easter eggs for the children. They also knock eggs in clenched fists, and have egg races in a game called **pace-egging**.

In the **Czech Republic**, they play an old game called **Pomlazka**. Boys chase the girls, and when they catch them they tap their legs lightly with willow twigs until the girls hand over a painted egg. 'Pomlazka!' shout the boys dancing around.

In **England**, mainly in the north of the country, the ceremony of **egg-rolling** is still to be seen at Easter time.

In Avenham Park, Preston, in Lancashire, egg-rolling or pace-egging is played by children, by rolling their hard-boiled eggs down the grassy slope. The first egg to reach the bottom is the winner. Defeated rivals have their eggs taken from them and eaten.

Some say that this tradition symbolises the rolling aside of the stone blocking the sepulchre from where Christ was resurrected.

But others say it is a simple game left over from ancient spring festivals, which involved more complicated egg rituals. These were performed to ensure the fields grew good crops.

The word '**pace**' isn't to do with the speed of the egg rolling down the hill. It comes from the world 'paschal', from the Hebrew '**Pesach**', for Passover.

'Here's two or three jolly children all of one mind,

We've come a pace-egging

And hope you'll be kind.

We hope you'll be kind

With your eggs and your hare,

And we'll come no more pace-egging

Until the next year.'

In **France**, church bells are silent from Maundy Thursday to Easter morning. The children are told that the bells have flown off to Rome to fetch them their eggs. When the bells return they'll be full of Easter eggs.

In **Germany**, green eggs are eaten on the Thursday before Easter. They dye the eggs by boiling them in spinach. The children put out little nests of moss so that the Easter rabbit can leave her eggs in it, safe from harm.

In **Greece**, people take candles to church at Easter time. The priest lights the candle of his neighbours, and this light is then passed from person to person until all the candles are lit. The peal of bells can be heard through the din of fireworks. The lighted candles are carefully carried home – the flame mustn't go out. Then everyone feasts on red-dyed hard-boiled eggs which are placed in a round loaf.

In **Ireland**, the story is told of how the robin came flying over Calvary on the Good Friday. The robin looked down at Jesus on the cross and saw that a thorn from the hawthorn crown had pierced the skin of his forehead.

So the robin swooped down, and plucked out the thorn with his beak. A drop of blood flowed out of the wound and stained the robin's breast. Since that day, the robin has had a red breast.

In **Florence**, **Italy**, a cart laden with fireworks and flowers is paraded through the streets. A firework dove flies from the cathedral and touches the cart, so igniting the fireworks.

In **Mexico** on Easter Saturday, papier mâché images of the traitor Judas appear attached to poles. They are filled with fireworks, which are lit. The explosion is the signal for rejoicing. Children also tie sticks together forming a cross. Then they weave brightly coloured wools into a diamond pattern. This is called 'The Eye of God'.

In **Sweden**, children dress up as Easter witches. They go from house to house holding a coffee pot into which people put sweets and coins. Branches of trees are brought into the house so that they will blossom on Easter Sunday. This has led to the custom of making an Easter tree. From the branches they hang decorated blown eggs. (See page 21.)

Things to do

Pysanky – Egg Decorating

Ukranians are particularly well known for the beautiful folk art 'pysanky', a craft passed down from generation to generation. They use a 'kistka' (a small writing instrument), a lighted candle, beeswax, and several jars of brilliant dyes. A finished design may take hours and have dozens of layers of wax and dyes. The eggs are raw and eventually dry out when left. The many intricate designs of the Ukranians are based on symbols; for example, wheat represents the bountiful harvest.

You will need:
eggs, a candle, food dye

Method
1. Hold a lighted candle over the egg allowing some wax to drip on it. (This becomes the light part of your design.)
2. Dip the egg into some dye until it turns the shade you want.
3. Add some more wax, and dip into a second colour. Remove the wax by rubbing it off with a cloth. You might need to warm the egg in the oven if the wax has become too hard.

Colouring Eggs with Natural Dyes

Red is probably the favourite colouring for Easter eggs – some say it represents the blood of Christ – but any colour can be used.

A quick test to see if an egg is stale or not is to fill a cup or glass with salty water. If the egg sinks to the bottom it's fine; if it floats to the top it is stale, so do not use it.

You will need:
eggs, an old pan, old rags, leaves or flowers, any of the following:
spinach: turns eggs yellowy-green;
beetroot: turns them red;
tea: dyes them dark brown;
onion skin: wrapped round eggs and secured with an old nylon stocking makes a golden yellow colour;
coffee grounds or the bark of plum or young oak trees: turns them brown;
food colouring: any colour

Method
1. Tie rags round the egg, together with some leaves or flowers. This will make interesting patterns.
2. Boil in an old pan with any of the suggested ingredients above. If using food colouring, add a few drops to the water.
3. Simmer for at least 10 minutes, then leave to cool in the dye.

Things to do

An Easter Egg Tree

You will need:
eggs, paint, sequins, small shells or flowers, varnish (optional), thread, small branch of a tree

Method
1. Make a tiny hole at either end of the egg. Blow slowly until the yolk emerges, then save this for cooking. Rinse under cool water, dry and decorate. You can varnish the eggs lightly.
2. Take the branch and plant it in a flower pot. Decorate the pot with coloured paper. Thread the eggs and hang them from the branches. You can also hang little chocolate eggs from the tree.

Eggshell Boat

There was once a belief that whenever a boiled egg was eaten the empty shell should be broken. This was to foil any witch who was waiting to steal the eggshell to use as a boat, so that she could head out to sea and brew a storm.

'You must break the shell to bits for fear
The witches should make it a boat, my dear;
For over the sea, away from home,
Far by night the witches roam.'

Papier Mâché Eggs

You will need:
round balloon, wallpaper paste (without fungicide, as this is harmful), water

Filling for the eggs:
Straw or strands of coloured paper, small chocolate Easter eggs, sweets or biscuits, small toys, or painted eggs.

Method
1. Blow up the balloon.
2. Mix wallpaper paste and water together as instructed. If you don't have any glue you can use 3 cups flour to 1 cup water, and mix them to a batter consistency.
3. Soak torn-up newspaper in glue or flour mixture.

Depending on the age group this can be a little messy, so with the smaller children, allow them to paint the glue on to the paper and then stick it on the balloon.
4. Cover the balloon with at least six layers of paper.
5. When the balloon is dry, cut in half by zig-zagging all the way round. Paint and decorate the egg. Use the straw to line the egg, then add the filling.

For smaller eggs make an egg-shaped ball of Plasticine instead of a balloon to use as a 'former'. Then follow the above instructions from 2 onwards.

In **Switzerland**, people roll eggs down the snowy mountainsides. The parents whistle on Easter morning for the Easter hare, who then is said to come secretly into the house and hide eggs in small baskets for the children to find.

In the **United States**, thousands of people arrive at the White House, where they are allowed to roll their hard-boiled eggs across the President's lawn. There is a competition to see whose egg goes the furthest. Adults are only allowed in if they are accompanied by a child. Dolly Madison, the wife of one of the presidents, began this ritual in 1877.

Who is the Easter Hare?

Originally the Easter hare was the sacred companion of the goddess Eastre, whose festival was in spring.

This is how the hare was associated with Easter. Parents told their children that the magic hare would run through the night and bring them presents. So now in many places children prepare little nests in the garden, ready to receive the eggs brought by the Easter hare.

In some countries, people confused the hares with rabbits, and that is why the Easter rabbit has completely taken over from the original hare.

Why should it be the hare bringing the eggs when birds lay them?

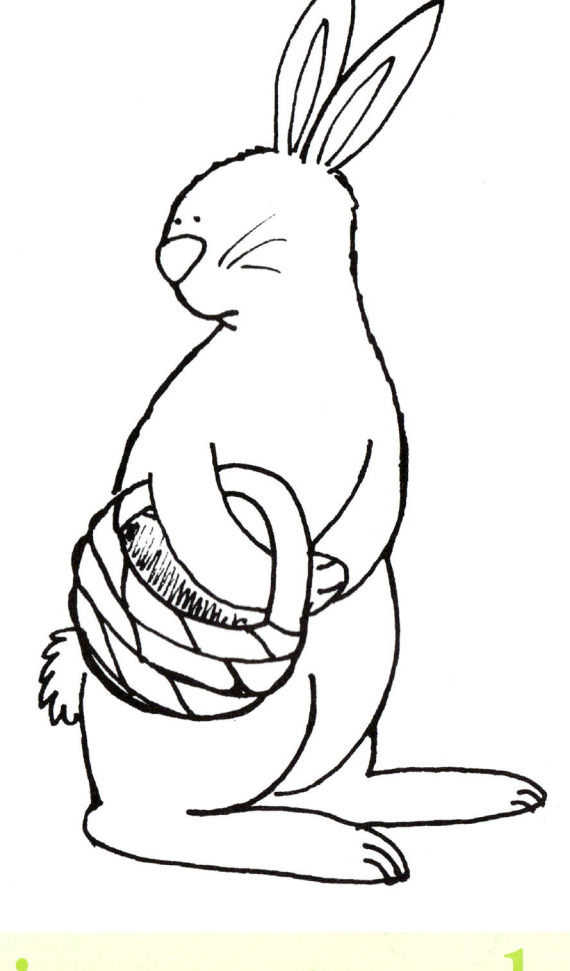

Things to do

1000-Year-Old Eggs

These eggs, when peeled, have a lovely marble design and can be eaten. Use other dyes for different effects.

You will need:
three eggs, two teabags

Method
1. Place the eggs in a saucepan of cold water and boil gently for 10 minutes. Cool under a cold tap.
2. Tap the eggs gently all over on a hard surface, cracking the egg slightly all over.
3. Boil the eggs and teabags together for 10 minutes.

When you peel them, they will have a lovely marble design and you can eat them. If you want different effects, use other colour dyes.

Surprise Eggs

You will need:
card, paper fasteners

Method
1. Cut out two identical egg shapes – 20cm from top to base.
2. Draw a surprise monster, or a scary face, or a baby creature on one.
3. Decorate and zig-zag cut the other.
4. Paper fasten the two halves to the top and bottom of the base – these can then be swivelled to reveal the surprise.

Cooking for Easter

Simnel Cake

The traditional gift of a simnel cake was made with **simeda** which is a fine wheat flour. It is rich, well-spiced and covered with almond paste. Recipes can be found on page 43.

Koulich

This is a traditional cake eaten during Easter time in Russia and known as Pashka, a 'tall cake', or koulich. The Russian initials KV, standing for Khristos Voskress, are printed on the frosting. See page 42 for how to make them.

Chicken Buns for Easter

In Norway, they make chicken buns for Easter. Recipe on page 41.

Easter Cakes

In the UK, they make Easter cakes and Easter biscuits. Recipes on page 44.

The Chickens

Said the first little chicken
    With a queer little squirm,
'I wish I could find
    A fat little worm.'

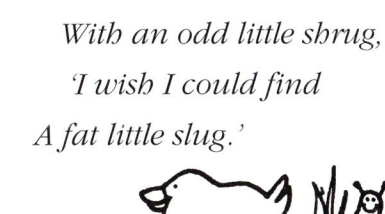

Said the next little chicken
    With an odd little shrug,
'I wish I could find
    A fat little slug.'

Said the third little chicken
    With a sharp little squeal,
'I wish I could find
    Some nice yellow meal.'

Said the fourth little chicken
    With a small sigh of grief,
'I wish I could find
    A little green leaf.'

Said the fifth little chicken
    With a faint little moan,
'I wish I could find
    A wee gravel stone.'

'Now see here' said the mother,
    From the green garden patch,
'If you want
    any breakfast
Just come here
    and scratch.'

Anon.

April

'April brings the primrose sweet,

Scatters daisies at our feet.'

The season of spring sprinkles the earth with soft showers, and calls up its flowers so slight and pretty.

This month of beauty and new birth, when the earth wakes from its winter sleep, when the buds appear on branches and the woods are full of song, is called April, the opener. The Romans saw that this month opened the gates of birth and restored to life all those lovely and gentle things which had hidden in terror from the blasts of winter.

The Four Seasons • Spring

April

Two little clouds one April day,
Went sailing across the sky.
They went so fast, and bumped their heads,
And both began to cry.

The big round sun came out and said,
'Oh, never mind, my dears,
I'll send all my sunbeams down,
To dry your fallen tears.'

Anon.

Things to do

Grow a Name

You will need:
mustard and cress seeds, kitchen towel, cotton wool, two small trays, water

Method
1. Place the cotton wool between two sheets of kitchen towel on a tray. Sprinkle the cress seeds to form a name, and moisten with the water.
2. Do the same on the second tray using the mustard seed, and see which one grows first.
3. The seeds take around 2 weeks to grow. Make sure the seeds are kept moist, but don't drown them.

Cress Potato People

You will need:
cress seeds, large potato, felt tips, water

Method
1. Slice the top off the potato and pierce the top with a fork, ready for the seeds.
2. Slice the bottom so the potato can stand. Draw a face on the potato with the felt tips. At the top of the potato plant the seeds.

When we did this at school, it took almost three weeks for the shoots to appear. Matthew, aged three, took his home, planted it, and in no time at all, he proudly returned to school clutching his plant with beans growing on it.

Broad Bean

You will need:
broad bean soaked overnight, blotting paper, labels, jar, plant pot

Method
1. Cut the blotting paper to the size of the jar and place inside. Pour a little water into the jar until the blotting paper is well soaked.
2. Push the bean between the jar and paper. Label the jars with each child's name. Place near a sunny window and keep moist.

April Fool's Day

Tricks have been played on 1 April for a long, long time, and in many different parts of the world.

People young and old have great fun playing tricks on April Fool's Day – changing the clocks perhaps, or getting a friend to ring a number and ask to speak to Mr C. Lion, the number being that of the local zoo! Even the newspapers run fun stories trying to trick the public. However, all fooling must end at midday, or else the joke is on the joker.

Some people think April Fool's Day dates back to 1582 when Pope Gregory's new-style calendar was accepted. New Year's Day moved from 1 April to 1 January but news did not travel fast in those days. Some people heard the news very late and were called **April Fool** or **April Fish**.

Some people say that the custom of making April Fools comes from the Roman festival **Cereali**, commemorating Ceres, the goddess of agriculture and the mother of Persephone.

In **France,** April Fool's Day is called **Poisson d'Avril** (April Fish) and the children stuff paper fish down each other's shirts.

In **India,** April Fool's Day takes place on 31 March and is called **Huli**.

In **Scotland,** an April Fool is called a **gowk**, the Gaelic word for cuckoo. This bird fools other birds by laying her eggs in their nests. She then leaves it up to the other bird to hatch her young. When the young cuckoo has hatched, it will toss the other birds out of the nest so that it can get the food from its foster-parents.

Today's The Day

Today's the day for having fun,
   Playing tricks on everyone.
Spiders in coffee and flies in the tea,
   Let's hang spaghetti from a tree.

Today's the day, April first,
Blowing up balloons and letting them burst.
Worms in sandwiches, slugs in the cake,
Let's see what mischief we can make.

By Shirley West

Things to do

April Fool Flowers

It's a fun way of seeing how flowers drink. An extension to this experiment is to use celery in place of the flowers and to see the veins of the celery suck up coloured water.

You will need:
a jar, water, food dye, some white flowers

Method
1. Mix ten drops of food dye with a little water in a jar. Cut the flower stems to just above the height of the jar. Leave in the water for a day or so.
2. Split the stem of the flower half-way up. Put one half in red dye and the other half in blue.

The Four Seasons • Spring

13 April
Baisakhi

Baisakhi, meaning 'April', is the beginning of the new year in India. The celebration is especially important to the Sikhs. In 1699 Guru Gobind Singh wanted to make the Sikhs' faith so strong that they would never denounce it. The guru held a meeting and called for someone who was prepared to give his life for the faith. Daya Ram, who was amongst the crowd, volunteered. The guru took him into a tent and appeared a few minutes later with a blood-stained sword, and then he called for four more volunteers. From the frightened crowd four more men came forward and were taken inside the tent. It was believed that the five men had been killed, but later they reappeared alive, dressed in shining yellow clothes and decorated with weapons.

The guru called these men **Panj Pyare** (Five Beloved Sikhs) and gave them the surname **Singh** ('Lion'). He called the group **Khalsa** ('The Pure Ones') and baptised them with **amrit**, which is made from sugar and water. He then ordered them to maintain five symbols of the faith. These were:

Kesh: uncut hair

Kangha: a comb to fix the hair

Kara: a steel bracelet worn on the right wrist

Kirpan: a short sword

Kachh: the shorts

The turban and these five articles form a uniform which all Sikhs wear.

Baisakhi is a time when Sikhs who wish to join the fellowship of the Khalsa are baptised at a ceremony called **Amri Chakna**.

Baisakhi lasts for three days, two of which are spent in prayer, singing hymns and giving speeches. On the third day, the congregation gathers for the sharing of fruit and **karah parshad** (ghee, flour, milk and sugar). The festival ends with two dances, the **bhangra** danced by the men, and the **giddha** danced by the women. After the ceremony they all eat a vegetarian meal.

Things to do

A Bracelet from Baker's Clay

You will need:
4 cups of flour, 1 cup of salt, ½ cup of water, a thin knitting needle, thin elastic
Oven temperature: 180°C/350°F/Gas 4

Method
1. Mix flour, salt and water together. Knead until firm.
2. Mould the baker's clay into round bead shapes. Make a hole right through each bead with the knitting needle.
3. Carefully place the beads on a baking tray. Bake in the oven for about 1 hour, until lightly brown and firm to the touch.
4. Once the clay has cooled, the children can paint it. For a harder finish, coat with varnish. Then thread the beads with elastic and tie to form a bracelet.

May

'May brings flocks of pretty lambs, Sporting round their fleecy dams.'

The Greek goddess **Maia** gave her name to the month of May. Maia was thought to encourage growth. In her honour, sacrifices were made on the first day of May, accompanied by dancing and merrymaking. Maia has a famous father, Atlas, who is thought to carry the world on his shoulders.

The Anglo-Saxons called this month **thir-milci** ('three-milk'), because the grass became more plentiful, and so the cows were able to give milk three times a day.

May Day

At the beginning of May, the Romans used to honour Flora, their goddess of vegetation and flowers. They decorated a tree or maypole, then danced and feasted round it. They brought these customs to Britain, and the maypole became an essential part of the springtime activities.

In medieval times, 1 May was celebrated in England by crowning a May Queen and dancing round a maypole. The Lord of the May, now rarely seen, was once as important as the May Queen. Silk handkerchiefs were tied round his legs and arms, such as morris dancers still wear today. He carried a sword and was completely covered with greenery. He was called Jack-in-the-Green or Jack-in-the-Bush. He was adopted by chimney sweeps, whose annual holiday was on May Day. His name lives on in the sign boards of many pubs called 'The Green Man'.

Preparations for May Day were made the night before, when young people would go out into the countryside and return with armfuls of flowers and greenery with which to decorate the maypole and the cottages in the village. Maypoles were frequently made of hawthorn, a tree which symbolised joy at the return of summer.

A May Queen and attendants are often chosen to reign over the day's merrymaking. They originally represented Flora and her Nymphs. In later centuries the Christian church made links between May and Mary, and then celebrations became religious in tone. Roman Catholics still honour Mary with the title **Queen of May** and have dedicated the month to her.

In **England**, May Day ceremonies are held at places such as Ickwell Green. Children sing traditional songs, and dance. The men can be seen wearing smocks, and the women wear ankle-length dresses. Two **moggies** collect money in strange costumes, blackened faces and carrying brooms.

The maypole on Ickwell's village green is a permanent structure, and dancing around it is one of the highlights of the festival. A May Queen is selected from one of the three villages which take part in the celebration: Ickwell, Caldecote, and Warden.

In **Russia** along the avenues reaching out from Red Square the buildings are decorated with colourful mosaics of gigantic statues of labourers. Since the workers were considered the most important people of the Soviet Union, a special holiday, May Day, honoured them. In Moscow there are parades which usually begin as small neighbourhood groups, finally converging in Red Square in a colourful mass of flags and flowers. In St Petersburg the focal point of May Day is the Winter Palace of the Czars.

Things to do

May Day Basket

In New England, in the United States, May Day baskets are filled with sweets and fresh flowers. They are left on the doorstep of a friend, or hung on the doorknob. The bell is then rung, and the child runs away or hides before he or she is caught.

You will need:
4 cups of plain flour, 1 cup of salt, 1 ½ cups of water, a pudding bowl, tissue paper, ribbon
Oven temperature: 200°C/400°F/Gas 6

Method
1. Mix flour, salt and water, kneading it until firm. Roll the dough into a large circle.

2. Grease the outside of the pudding bowl. Carefully place dough around the bowl. Make a hole either side ready for the ribbon. Bake for an hour until lightly brown and firm.

3. Remove the pastry from the bowl and cool. Place the tissue paper all around it. Tie the ribbon through the holes.

Japanese Boys' Day

5 May

Kodomo-no-hi, or **Tango-no-sekkhu**, is a festival for children and a national holiday. Originally it was a festival for boys only. Families with boys put up **koinobori**, or carp streamers, in their gardens and display their Samaurai warrior dolls called **gogatsuningyo** indoors. A banner for each boy in the family is made in the shape of a carp fish and painted with bright colours.

The eldest son normally has the largest banner. The symbol of the carp is chosen because this fish is so strong and brave that it can leap a waterfall and it swims vigorously against the current. Parents hope to see the same qualities in their children. The sword-shaped iris leaf, being symbolic of the spirit of brave warriors, is placed in the boy's bath water.

Things to do

The Koinobori

These are banners in the shape of a colourful carp and made of cloth and paper.

The top banner is called 'fukinagashi', which means the pennant. The next is called 'magoi', a black carp, representing the father of the house. Then comes 'higoi', a red carp, for the mother. Smaller carps are attached, one for each son.

A Carp Fish for the Koinobori

You will need:
a long balloon, newspaper, paste, card, paint, differently coloured paper, a long pole

Method
1. Tear newspaper into strips and paste several layers on to the balloon to form the carp's body. Cut the card into fin shapes and mould to the fish's body using glued newspaper. Allow to dry for 24 hours.
2. Cut out the front of the balloon to form the carp's mouth. Make a small hole for the pole above and below the jaw, then paint. Allow to dry.
3. Cut the coloured paper into oval shapes and long streamers. Glue the oval shapes all over the carp's body. Then glue the streamers at the end, and along the carp's back.
4. When it is dry attach the fish to the pole.

Cooking Mochi

'Mochi' are glutinous rice cakes eaten in Japan. They are produced by pounding glutinous rice in a large wooden pot. The chewy white paste that results is shaped into round cakes, and these are eaten as they are or lightly toasted. You'll find the recipe on page 44.

The Four Seasons • Spring

World health Day
7 April

The World Health Organisation (WHO) came into being on 7 April 1948. In 1977, WHO set a target of 'Health for All by the Year 2000'. In many Third World countries, lack of food is the major cause of death among children.

Food provides the body with the materials it needs to build and repair itself. It also provides the energy which fuels the body. A balanced, healthy diet is very important to maintaining good health.

In the Western world people eat too much 'junk' food, which does not always contain the healthy balance of proteins, minerals and fats which our bodies need.

Things to do

'Which Foods Are Good For Me?' Collage

Ask the children to think about which foods are good for them and which foods aren't good for them.

Collect wrappers from healthy and unhealthy foods and drinks. With the wrappers and cans make a collage. Entitle one side **Healthy Foods** and the other side **Unhealthy Foods.**

Make a collage of foods showing the different nutrients. Here is a list of some of them:

Carbohydrates produce energy, and are found in pasta, potato, beans, lentils, nuts, vegetables, fruit and grains.

Fats are found in dairy products, cooking oils and meat.

Proteins are found in pulses, cereals, cheese, bread, milk, fish, nuts, seeds, vegetables (peas, beans and lentils) and meats; they help the body grow and repair itself.

Fibre is found in cereals, brown bread, brown rice, baked beans, nuts, vegetables and fruit; it helps keep the digestive system in good order.

Minerals, such as iron (in bran, wheatgerm and parsley), magnesium (in Brazil nuts, peanuts and almonds) and calcium (in cheddar cheese, spinach and watercress), help with growth and repair, and are very important for strong bones and teeth.

Vitamins fall into two types: the fat-soluble vitamins which are found in fats and oils, meat, fish and dairy products; and water-soluble vitamins which are found in dairy products, cereals, fruit and vegetables. These, together with minerals, help to regulate the body processes.

Cooking

Muesli Munchies on page 44 make a very healthy snack.

Calendar

Sometime in February or March

Lent Monday (Christianity)
First day of Lent for the Eastern Orthodox Churches.

Shrove Tuesday (Christianity)
Christians seek forgiveness for their sins and prepare for Lent. A feast day associated with making and eating pancakes, in some parts of the world. In other places it is celebrated with carnivals and Mardi Gras.

Ash Wednesday (Christianity)
Marks the beginning of Lent – the period of contemplation and fasting in preparation for Easter.

1	**St David's Day (Christianity)**	St David is the patron saint of Wales.
3	**Hanamastsur Hina-matsuri (Shinto)**	The Japanese celebrate the birthday of Buddha Shaklyamuni with this floral festival; images of the Buddha are set in floral shrines and bathed.
11	**Purim (Judaism)**	Jews celebrate the bravery of Queen Esther who saved her people from destruction in Persia.
17	**St Patrick's Day (Christianity)**	St Patrick is the patron saint of Ireland.
21	**Jamshedi Noruz 'Baha'i & Zoroastrianism'**	New Year's Day for Baha'is and Zoroastrians.
22	**Holi (Hinduism)**	The most boisterous of India's festivals, which celebrates harvest and the earth's fertility; people throw coloured powder and water at each other, and it is a time for fun and dancing.

Calendar

Sometime in March or April

Palm Sunday (Christianity)
Celebrates the triumphant entry of Jesus into Jerusalem and marks the beginning of Holy Week. Crosses made of palm fronds are distributed in churches and hung in homes.

Passover (Pesach) (Judaism)
An eight-day festival which celebrates the Exodus of the Israelites from Egypt. An important feature of this festival is the Seder, which describes in words, songs and prayers and with traditional food the story of Exodus.

Maundy Thursday (Christianity)
Commemorates the Last Supper, i.e. the Institution of the Eucharist: in particular Jesus washing his disciples' feet.

Good Friday (Christianity)
Commemorates the crucifixion of Jesus. A solemn feast day, so called because Christians believe his death to be the highest example of self-sacrifice. Hot cross buns are associated with this day.

Easter Day (Christianity)
The most important festival of the Christian calendar. It celebrates the resurrection of Jesus from the dead. Easter eggs, relics of an earlier pagan feast, are associated with Easter; they are symbols of new life.

1	**April Fool's Day**	
3	**Ramanavami (Hinduism)**	Birthday of Lord Rama.
4–6	**Ching Ming (Taoism)**	The Chinese visit their family tombs at this time; graves are cleansed and offerings made to the spirits of their ancestors, to remember and respect the dead.
7	**World Health Day**	
13	**Baisakhi (Sikh)**	Commemorates the founding of the Khalsa, the Brotherhood of Sikhism by Gobind Singh, the tenth Guru.
14	**Hefful Day**	Cuckoo Day in England.
19	**Primrose Day**	
21	**Ridvan (Baha'i)**	The first day of a festival which commemorates Baha-u-llah's first declaration of his mission. The other important days of this 12-day feast are the 9th and 12th; Baha-u-llah is the founder of the Baha'i faith.
22	**Yom Hashoah (Judaism)**	Remembrance Day for the victims of the Nazi Holocaust.
23	**St George's Day (Christianity)**	St George is the patron saint of England.
30	**Yom ha'atzma'ut (Judaism)**	Celebrates Israel's independence.

Calendar

Sometime in May or June

Ascension Day (Christianity)
Commemorates Jesus's last appearance to his disciples and his ascension to heaven.

Whitsun/Pentecost (Christianity)
Sometimes called the birthday of the Christian church. It commemorates the time when the followers of Jesus received the Holy Spirit.

Wesak
Buddhist festival.

Shovout
The Jewish Pentecost.

1	**May Day**	
5	**Kodomo-no-ho**	Children's Day in Japan.
2nd Sunday		Mother's Day in the USA.
8	**Buddha purnima/Vesakpuja/ Parinirvana (Buddhism)**	A very important feast for Buddhists, celebrating the birthday, enlightenment and death of Buddha.
23	**Declaration of the Bab (Baha'i)**	Celebrates the declaration by Mirza Ali Muhammed of his mission as forerunner of Baha-u-llah, the founder of the Baha'i faith.
27	**Martyrdom of Guru Arjun Dev, fifth Guru and first Sikh martyr (Sikh)**	
28	**Dragon Boat Festival (Taoism)**	Famous for the dragon boat regatta, this festival is held in honour of China's great poet Qu Yuan. It is also a celebration of the victory of honour over evil as reflected in the teachings of Tao and Confucius.
29	**Ascension of Baha-u-llah**	Commemorates the ascension of the founder of the Baha'i faith.
30	**Shavuot (Judaism)**	Jews thank God on this day for the Ten Commandments and the Torah.

Calendar

Festivals of the Lunar Year

Ramadan (Islam)
Time of fasting and self-restraint for Muslims. It also commemorates the sending of the Qur'an to the world through its revelation to Mohammad. Zakat, or alms-giving, is an important feature of Ramadan.

Lailat-ul-Qadr (Islam)
Falls on the 27th day of Ramadan. The holiest of nights, which commemorates the beginning and the end of the revelation of the Qur'an to Mohammed.

Lailat-ul-barah (Islam)
The night of forgiveness: Muslims seek mutual forgiveness in preparation for Ramadan; they also believe that their destiny for the year is determined on this night.

Eid-ul-fitr (Islam)
The end of the fasting period of Ramadan; Zakat, or alms-giving, is an important part of the day's celebration.

The lunar year consists of 12 lunar months, and is only about 354 days long, so the dates of these festivals in the solar calendar move backwards by about 11 days each year.

Recipes

Bao Bing

You will need:
350g (12oz) flour
5ml (1 teaspoon) salt
120ml (½ cup) hot water
cooking oil
beansprouts

Method

1. Sift flour with salt. Add enough hot water (about ½ cup) to make soft dough.

2. Divide into 24 small balls. Flatten each ball until it is 5cm (2") in diameter.

3. Brush top one with oil and put another over it. Roll together with a rolling pin to make a pancake 15cm (6") in diameter. Repeat until there are 12 pancakes.

4. Heat a heavy pan and bake each pancake on both sides. Keep cooked pancakes wrapped in a cloth on a warmed dish.

5. Cook beansprouts in water for 5 minutes.

6. When ready to be eaten, peel each pancake into two. The oil layer will have allowed them to separate. Put a spoonful of the beansprouts and eggs on the pancake. Fold over one end and roll up.

Blini

You will need:
225g (8oz) flour
2 eggs
½ litre (17½ fl oz) milk
salt and sugar to taste
margarine for frying

Method

1. Mix all ingredients together to form a batter.

2. Heat margarine in a small frying pan and scoop enough batter to cover bottom of pan and cook either side.

3. Serve with melted butter and sour cream.

Pancakes

You will need:
110g (4oz) plain flour
large pinch of salt
1 egg
250ml (½ pt) liquid – half milk, half water
30ml (1 tablespoon) cooking oil
cooking oil for frying pancakes

Method

1. Sift flour and salt into a mixing bowl. Add egg and half the liquid. Beat to a smooth batter. Stir in rest of liquid and tablespoon of cooking oil; pour into a jug.

2. Heat a little oil to cover bottom of pan. Pour enough batter to coat pan thinly. Fry pancake briskly, then toss or turn and fry other side.

3. Turn out on to a plate and serve with castor sugar and lemon juice.

Recipes

Crêpes

You will need:
240ml (1 cup) water
240ml (1 cup) cold milk
4 eggs
2½ ml (½ teaspoon) salt
285g (10oz) sifted flour
60ml (4 tablespoons) melted butter
30-40ml (2-3 tablespoons) cooking oil

Method

1. Place all ingredients (except the oil) in blender, cover and blend at top speed for 1 minute.

2. Store in refrigerator for at least 2 hours.

3. Heat the oil in a skillet or crêpe pan before adding the batter.

4. Using ¼ cup batter per crêpe, fry quickly, shaking pan backwards and forwards to keep crêpe from sticking.

5. Once it has been tossed and browned quickly on other side, crêpe is ready to be filled with creamed chicken, cheese or mushrooms. For a dessert, fill crêpe with jam or ice cream and top with chocolate or strawberry sauce.

Hot Cross Buns

You will need:
7g (¼ oz) dried yeast
150ml (¼ pt) milk sweetened with 1 teaspoon sugar
340g (12oz) plain flour
5ml (1 teaspoon) salt
30g (1oz) margarine
55g (2oz) sugar
5ml (1 teaspoon) mixed spice
5ml (1 teaspoon) ground cinnamon
2½ ml (½ teaspoon) ground nutmeg
110g (4oz) currants
1 egg, beaten

Sugar glaze
5ml (1 teaspoon) sugar boiled with 15ml (1 tablespoon) water

Oven temperature: 220°C/425°F/Gas 7

Method

1. Activate yeast with sweetened milk.

2. Sieve flour and salt, rub in fat; add sugar, spices and fruit.

3. Add yeast and egg to dry ingredients. Use a little more milk if necessary to make a soft dough; cover and leave in a warm place to double in size.

4. Knead until smooth, divide into 12 pieces, shape into rounds, and place on greased baking trays. Mark each bun with a cross cut. Leave to prove for 15-20 minutes.

5. Cut crosses again and bake for about 15 minutes.

6. When cooked, brush with sugar glaze.

Recipes

Nan Bread

You will need:
200g (7oz) plain white flour
2½ ml (½ teaspoon) salt
5ml (1 teaspoon) baking powder
5ml (1 teaspoon) plain yoghurt
60g (2oz) butter
56ml (2 fl oz) water

Oven temperature:
190°C/375°F/Gas 5

Method

1. Sift flour, salt and baking powder into a bowl. Add yoghurt and half of the butter. Mix to a soft dough. Gradually add water.

2. Divide into 5 balls, cover and leave for 4 hours.

3. Knead each ball on a floured surface and roll out. Brush the circles with the remainder of the butter (melted) and place on a tray.

4. Cook in the oven on both sides for 4 minutes or until brown specks appear. They can also be shallow-fried.

Rice Biscuits

You will need:
110g (4oz) butter
225g (8oz) ground rice
salt to taste
225g (8oz) sugar
5ml (1 teaspoon) ground nutmeg
½ cup milk

Oven temperature: 180°C/350°F/Gas 4

Method

1. Mix butter and ground rice together. Add salt and sugar dissolved in a little water. Add nutmeg and milk.

2. Knead to a stiff dough. Take a large portion of dough and roll out to biscuit thickness.

3. Cut out dough with a biscuit cutter, or make flower shapes, and place on a greased tray.

4. Bake until golden brown.

Phirni

You will need:
450ml (16 fl oz) milk
30g (1oz) ground rice
110g (4oz) sugar to taste
few drops vanilla essence
10ml (2 teaspoons) almonds (blanched, sliced and fried until light brown)
10ml (2 teaspoons) raisins

Method

1. Bring milk to the boil. Add ground rice and sugar; stir gently until it thickens.

2. Stir in vanilla essence and pour into a greased baking tray. Decorate with almonds and raisins.

3. When cold, cut into squares.

Recipes

Phuluka

You will need:
280g (10oz) wholewheat flour
salt to taste
water
oil for cooking
margarine for serving

Method

1. Mix flour and salt together and make a soft dough with the water. Allow to stand for half an hour.

2. Knead well, and form into small balls. Roll out into small circles.

3. Fry in oil on either side until tiny blisters appear. Remove from the pan.

4. Spread with a little margarine and serve hot.

Pesach Rolls

You will need:
85g (3oz) margarine
225ml (8 fl oz) boiling water
285g (10oz) medium matzo meal
5ml (1 teaspoon) salt
5ml (1 teaspoon) sugar
4 eggs

Oven temperature: 180°C/350°F/Gas 4

Method

1. Melt fat in the water and bring to the boil.

2. Add all the dry ingredients and beat until mixture forms a ball and leaves the side of the pan clean.

3. Beat in eggs one at a time. Beat mixture hard for 1 minute.

4. Place on greased trays. Bake until well risen and brown.

Matzo Pudding

You will need:
3 matzos
110g (4oz) fine matzo meal
110g (4oz) sultanas
110g (4oz) sugar
55g (2oz) ground almonds
55g (2oz) currants
2 eggs
15ml (1 teaspoon) cinnamon or mixed spice
grated rind and juice of 1 lemon
15ml (1 tablespoon) margarine or fat for baking

Oven temperature: 170°C/325°F/Gas 3

Method

1. Soak matzos until soft. Squeeze very dry and put in bowl.

2. Add remaining ingredients (except fat), and mix well.

3. Melt fat in a baking dish and add mixture. Bake in a moderate oven for about 1 hour.

Recipes

Orange and Lemon Squash

You will need:
900g (2lb) granulated sugar
860ml (1½ pt) water
juice and grated rind of 3 large lemons
juice and grated rind of 2 large oranges
20ml (4 level teaspoons) tartaric acid

Method

1. Dissolve sugar and water in a pan, and bring to boil. Simmer for 10 minutes.

2. Place lemon and orange rind in a bowl with tartaric acid; pour in the sugar syrup, mixing well.

3. Cover and leave to stand for 24 hours.

4. Strain in the lemon and orange juice. Pour the squash into bottles and seal. Store in a cool place and dilute to taste with water.

Orange and Lemon Biscuits

You will need:
110g (4oz) butter or margarine
110g (4oz) caster sugar
1 egg (beaten)
rind of 1 orange or lemon
225g (8oz) plain flour
icing sugar
orange or lemon colouring
hot water

Oven temperature: 180°C/350°F/Gas 4

Method

1. Cream butter and sugar together. Add egg and citrus rind a little at a time. Beat after each addition.

2. Stir in flour and mix to a fairly firm dough. Cut into orange and lemon shapes.

3. Place on greased baking tray. Bake in the centre of the oven. Allow to cool.

4. Make icing for the biscuits by mixing icing sugar with colouring and hot water.

Recipes

Chicken Buns

You will need:

yeast
450g (1lb) strong bread flour
5ml (1 teaspoon) salt
small knob butter
about 300ml (½ pt) lukewarm milk
currants, red glacé cherries for decoration
1 egg (beaten)

Method

1. Ferment yeast. Add slowly to the flour, salt and butter and milk in a bowl. Knead dough vigorously.

2. Divide into 12 equal pieces. Roll each piece into a fat snake about 10cm long. Make a knot in each snake.

3. Push in two currants for eyes and a piece of red glacé cherry for a beak.

4. Place on a greased baking sheet and cover with a piece of greased polythene. Leave in a warm place for at least an hour until they double in size.

5. Brush gently with beaten egg and bake in a very hot oven for 5–10 minutes.

Raisin Bars

You will need:

4 eggs (separated)
110g (4oz) sugar
30ml (2 tablespoons) water
110g (4oz) plain flour
2½ ml (½ teaspoon) salt
½ grated rind of lemon
110g (4oz) chopped almonds
110g (4oz) raisins

Oven temperature: 180°C/350°F/Gas 4

Method

1. Beat yolks and sugar until light.

2. Add water, flour, salt and lemon rind. Stir in almonds and raisins.

3. Fold stiffly-beaten egg whites.

4. Place in greased round tin and cut into 8 sections. Bake for 30 minutes or until brown.

Recipes

Easter Biscuits

This recipe will make 20-30 little biscuits.

You will need:
110g (4oz) butter or margarine
110g (4oz) caster sugar
1 egg, separated
225g (8oz) self-raising flour
pinch of salt
55g (2oz) currants
30g (1oz) mixed peel
20-30ml (1-2 tablespoons) milk

Oven temperature: 200°C/400°F/Gas 6

Method

1. Cream butter and sugar. Beat in egg yolk.

2. Sift the flour with the salt and fold into the creamed mixture. Add currants and mixed peel.

3. Add enough milk to make a fairly soft dough, cover and leave in a cool place to become firm.

4. Knead lightly on a floured board and roll out to 6mm (¼") thickness.

5. Cut into rounds, using a biscuit cutter. Put on a greased baking tray in the centre of the oven.

6. After about 10 minutes, brush the biscuits with the egg white, sprinkle with sugar and continue cooking for another 10 minutes.

Koulich

You will need:
110g (4oz) margarine
110g (4oz) sugar
1 egg (beaten)
225g (8oz) self-raising flour
55g (2oz) raisins
30g (1oz) chopped walnuts
110g (4oz) chopped candied fruits
vanilla essence
sugar icing
sugar confetti and silver balls for decoration

Oven temperature: 180°C/350°F/Gas 4

Method

1. Cream margarine and sugar together.

2. Add beaten egg and mix well.

3. Sift and fold in flour.

4. Add the raisins, nuts, candied fruits (reserving a few for decoration) and a dash of vanilla essence.

5. Pour batter into two round, well-greased baking tins and bake for 1 hour.

6. Let cake cool after baking, then spread icing over the top and add decorations.

The Four Seasons • Spring

Recipes

Simnel Cake

You will need:
225g (8oz) plain flour
pinch salt
large pinch of baking powder
55g (2oz) rice flour
225g (8oz) sultanas
110g (4oz) currants (washed)
110g (4oz) glacé cherries
30g (1oz) candied peel (finely chopped)
225g (8oz) butter
grated rind of 2 lemons
225g (8oz) caster sugar
4 eggs (separated)
almond paste
sieved icing sugar

Oven temperature: 150°C/300°F/Gas 2

Method

1. Sift flour, salt, baking powder and rice flour into a bowl.

2. Mix sultanas, currants, cherries and peel together.

3. Cream butter with the lemon rind until soft.

4. Add the sugar and continue creaming until mixture is light and fluffy. Beat in egg yolks.

5. Whip egg white until stiff.

6. Fold one-third of flour into mixture, then fold in egg whites alternately with remaining flour and fruit. Pour half the mixture into prepared tin, spreading it a little up the sides.

7. Make almond paste and divide it into three equal parts. Take the first portion, roll into a smooth round and place in tin. Cover with rest of cake mixture.

8. Bake in oven for 2 hours, then reduce heat to 140°C/275°F/Gas 1 and continue cooking for about 30 minutes, or until a skewer inserted in the cake comes out clean.

9. Allow to cool, then remove the cake from the tin and slide it onto a baking sheet.

10. Use the second portion of the almond paste to cover the top of the cake and the remainder to make 12 small balls to decorate the cake, as shown. Dust with icing sugar.

Almond Paste

You will need:
225g (8oz) ground almonds
285g (10oz) caster sugar
170g (6oz) sieved icing sugar
2 egg yolks, or 1 whole egg
juice of half a lemon
25–30ml (1-2 teaspoons) orange flower water

Method

1. Place almonds, castor sugar and icing sugar in a bowl and mix together.

2. Whisk egg yolk (or whole egg) with the lemon juice and flavouring. Add to the mixture of ground almonds and sugar.

3. Pound remainder of paste lightly to release a little of the oil from almonds. Knead paste with hands until smooth.

Recipes

Easter Cakes

You will need:

110g (4oz) margarine
110g (4oz) sugar
1 egg (beaten)
225g (8oz) self-raising flour
pinch of salt
2½ml (½ teaspoon) allspice
55g (2oz) currants

Oven temperature: 180°C/350°F/Gas 4

Method

1. Beat margarine and sugar until creamy.
2. Add beaten egg and mix well.
3. Sift in flour, salt and allspice.
4. Add currants and stir until well mixed.
5. Spoon into paper cake cases and bake for about 20 minutes.

Muesli Munchies

You will need:

110g (4oz) margarine
170g (6oz) raw cane sugar
1 large egg
110g (4oz) self-raising wholemeal flour
110g (4oz) oats
55g (2oz) raisins
55g (2oz) chopped nuts, raw or roasted
a little milk

Oven temperature: 180°C/350°F/Gas 4

Method

1. Cream margarine and sugar; add egg.
2. Mix in flour slowly.
3. Add remaining ingredients with milk to make a batter.
4. Drop tablespoons of the mixture onto a greased tray, leaving room for the biscuits to spread, and cook for 10–15 minutes.

Sweet Mochi

You will need:

255g (9oz) rice
570ml (1pt) water
salt
15ml (1 tablespoon) sugar or honey
56ml (2 fl oz) dark soy sauce
30g (1oz) sesame seeds

Method

1. Wash rice well and soak in cooking water for 1 hour. Boil with a little salt until very soft.
2. Allow rice to cool before kneading and pounding. Shape into small balls. These will be a close approximation to rice cakes.
3. Dissolve sugar or honey and soy sauce in saucepan over low heat. Pour into small bowl.
4. Toast sesame seeds, crush with rolling pin and spread in saucer.
5. Grill rice cakes for 2–3 minutes either side so that they soften and swell.
6. Dip rice cakes in soy sauce and honey mixture, then into sesame seeds.